Crabapples

Butterflies and Moths

Bobbie Kalman & Tammy Everts

Crabtree Publishing Company

Crabapples

created by Bobbie Kalman

for my aunt Marika

Editor-in-Chief
Bobbie Kalman

Writing team
Bobbie Kalman
Tammy Everts

Managing editor
Lynda Hale

Editors
Petrina Gentile
Janine Schaub

Illustrations
Barb Bedell: pages 14, 27
Antoinette "Cookie" DeBiasi:
    pages 5, 9, 12, 22-23
Tammy Everts: page 15

Color separations and film
Dot 'n Line Image Inc.

Printer
Worzalla Publishing Company

Computer design
Lynda Hale
David Schimpky

Photographs
Gerald & Buff Corsi/Tom Stack & Associates: page 10
John Daly: back cover, title page, page 12 (right), 19 (bottom),
    27 (top), 28 (top), 29 (top)
David M. Dennis/Tom Stack & Associates: page 11 (bottom), 21
Chip & Jill Eisenhart/Tom Stack & Associates: page 20
John Gerlach/Visuals Unlimited: front cover, page 24 (top)
A. Kerstitch/Visuals Unlimited: pages 25 (top), 29 (bottom)
Diane Payton Majumdar: pages 5, 6, 8 (top), 9 (bottom left), 15, 17,
    18 (bottom), 19 (top), 26 (both), 27 (bottom)
Jim McCullagh/Visuals Unlimited: page 23
John A. McDonald: pages 8 (bottom left and right), 9 (bottom right),
    12 (left), 13, 24 (bottom), 25 (bottom), 28 (bottom right)
Don & Esther Phillips/Tom Stack & Associates: page 18 (top)
N. Piluke/Visual Contact: page 28 (bottom left)
Rod Planck/Tom Stack & Associates: page 11 (top)
Milton Rand/Tom Stack & Associates: pages 7, 14
Kjell B. Sandved/Visuals Unlimited: page 16
Larry Tackett/Tom Stack & Associates: page 4
Roy Toft/Tom Stack & Associates: page 30

Crabtree Publishing Company

350 Fifth Avenue
Suite 3308
New York
N.Y. 10118

360 York Road, RR 4
Niagara-on-the-Lake
Ontario, Canada
L0S 1J0

73 Lime Walk
Headington
Oxford OX3 7AD
United Kingdom

Cataloging in Publication Data
Kalman, Bobbie, 1947-
    Butterflies and moths

(Crabapples)
Includes index.

ISBN 0-86505-614-5 (library bound) ISBN 0-86505-714-1 (pbk.)
This book examines aspects of butterflies and moths, including
metamorphosis, senses, coloration, and behavior.

1. Butterflies - Juvenile literature. 2. Moths - Juvenile
literature. I. Everts, Tammy, 1970-   . II. Title. III. Series:
Kalman, Bobbie, 1947-   . Crabapples.

QL544.2.K35 1994   j595.78   LC 94-5311
                                                                CIP

What is in this book?

What are butterflies and moths?　5

Moth or butterfly?　6

From egg to adult　8

Crawling caterpillars　10

What do butterflies and moths eat?　12

Using their senses　14

Beware of predators!　16

Colors that protect　18

Hiding from enemies　21

Sleep or fly away?　22

Unusual butterflies　24

Magnificent moths　26

The name game　29

Butterfly fun　30

Words to know & Index　31

What is in the picture?　32

What are butterflies and moths?

Butterflies and moths are insects. Insects have three body parts: a head, thorax, and abdomen. Insects have six legs. Many insects have wings. Butterflies and moths have large wings that are covered in tiny scales. The scales look like dust when they rub off on your fingers.

Butterflies and moths are important. They help plants grow by spreading pollen. They are food for many animals.

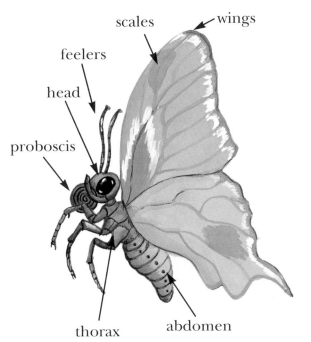

scales

wings

feelers

head

proboscis

thorax

abdomen

Moth or butterfly?

Butterflies and moths are alike. Sometimes it is difficult to tell them apart. Look at these two pictures. Which is the butterfly? Which is the moth?

Moth	Butterfly
thick, furry body	slender, hairless body
folds wings beside body when resting	brings wings up over body
usually smaller than a butterfly	usually larger than a moth
usually dull colored	usually brightly colored
usually flies at night	usually flies during the day

One easy way to tell if an insect is a butterfly or a moth is by looking at its feelers. A moth's feelers can be many shapes and sizes, but a butterfly's feelers are always long and slender with a knob on the tip.

1

The female butterfly or moth lays her eggs on a plant that will make good food for her young.

From egg to adult

Butterflies and moths start out as eggs. They grow into adults in a series of changes called **metamorphosis**. There are four changes in metamorphosis: egg, larva, pupa, and adult. These pictures show the cecropia moth as it grows and changes.

2

After a short time, each egg hatches into a caterpillar, or **larva**. The new caterpillar is very tiny, but it grows fast.

2a

The caterpillar soon gets too big for its skin. It sheds its tight skin and grows a new one. It does this several times.

The flying cecropia moth is an awesome sight!

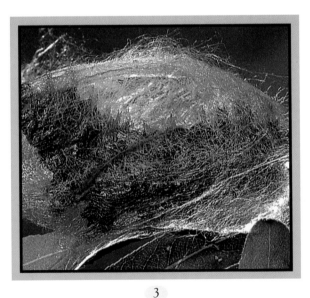

3

4

The caterpillar spins a cocoon around itself and is now called a **pupa**. Inside the **chrysalis**, the pupa changes into an adult.

Eventually, the adult breaks a hole in the cocoon and comes out. It rests its wings before it flies away.

Crawling caterpillars

It is hard to believe that a graceful butterfly or moth was once a crawling caterpillar. The word caterpillar means "hairy cat." Some caterpillars are covered with harmless fuzz. Others, such as this yellow-spotted tiger moth caterpillar, have long, stiff hairs or spines that can sting if you touch them.

A caterpillar looks as if it has dozens of legs. Like all insects, caterpillars have only six true legs. These are found at the front of the body. The rest of the caterpillar's "legs" are stumps called **prolegs**. Prolegs help the caterpillar cling to leaves and branches.

A swallowtail butterfly caterpillar has a red, orange, or yellow **osmeterium** on the top of its head. The osmeterium looks like a pair of horns. When the caterpillar is frightened, it pokes the horns at its enemy. The horns keep enemies away because they smell really bad!

What do butterflies and moths eat?

Adult moths and butterflies can only eat liquid food. Most sip **nectar**. Nectar is a sweet juice that is found inside flowers.

Butterflies and moths have a long tongue, called a **proboscis**, for drinking nectar. It works like a drinking straw. The proboscis is usually curled up, but it straightens when the insect eats.

uncurled proboscis

curled proboscis

Moth and butterfly caterpillars are nonstop eating machines! Most eat the leaves and stems of plants. Some eat only one type of plant. Others eat fruit, wool, wood, or wax. A few even eat other insects.

Using their senses

Butterflies and moths see, smell, taste, and hear differently than people do.

Butterflies and moths do not have noses. They use their feelers to smell!

Butterflies and moths eat with their proboscis, but they taste food with their feet!

Most butterflies and moths do not have ears, but some moths have very sensitive ears.

Butterflies and moths have **compound eyes**. Compound eyes have many flat sides, called **facets**. Each facet sees a separate picture. Compound eyes are very good at seeing movement. They can see some colors such as yellow, green, and blue, but they cannot see all the colors that our eyes can see.

compound eye

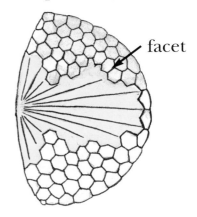

facet

Beware of predators!

Butterflies and moths have many **predators**. A predator is something that hunts another living thing. Snakes, toads, bats, spiders, and birds all eat butterflies and moths.

One type of wasp attaches its eggs to the caterpillar's body. When the eggs hatch, the baby wasps eat the caterpillar's insides while it is still alive! Then they build cocoons on the caterpillar's body.

17

Colors that protect

Butterflies and moths have special ways to protect themselves from animals that would like to eat them. Some have bright colors to frighten predators. The bright colors of others are a sign that they are poisonous. Their colors say "You will not like the way I taste!" or "I am much bigger than you think I am!"

Some butterflies, moths, and caterpillars have large **eyespots** on their wings or bodies. A spicebush swallowtail caterpillar's eyespots make it resemble a snake! The polyphemus moth's eyespots fool birds. Birds see the big false eyes and think they belong to a much larger animal.

Some harmless butterflies and moths are the same bright colors as poisonous butterflies and moths. These imitators, or **mimics**, have a "poisonous" look to fool their predators.

Can you tell the difference between these two butterflies? Animals cannot tell the difference either! The top one is a poisonous monarch, and the bottom one is a harmless viceroy.

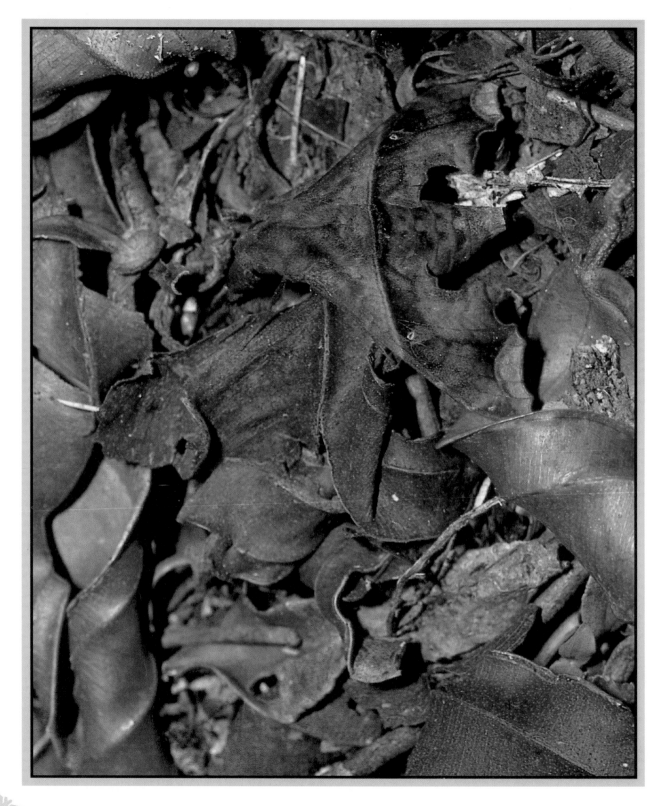

Hiding from enemies

Some insects use patterns and colors to hide from enemies. Patterns and colors help them blend into their environment. This blending is called **camouflage**.

Spot the hidden leaf-mimic moth on the opposite page. The moth's wings look exactly like withered brown leaves.

The caterpillar of the giant swallowtail butterfly is an unusual mimic. It looks just like a fresh bird dropping. Would birds want to eat this caterpillar?

Sleep or fly away?

Few butterflies and moths can live in freezing weather. Many die when the weather gets cold. Some butterflies and moths sleep through the winter as a pupa. This long rest is called **hibernation**. Other butterflies and moths fly hundreds or even thousands of miles to warmer places. This long flight is called **migration**.

The monarch butterfly has strong wings. At the end of every summer, it makes a long journey to the country of Mexico. Millions of monarch butterflies fly to the same part of Mexico every year. Hundreds of trees are completely covered with resting butterflies! Scientists do not know why monarch butterflies return to this place each year.

Unusual butterflies

There are over 20,000 kinds of butterflies in the world. Some are more unusual than others. The giant swallowtail is among the largest in North America. It is as big as an adult's hand! The pygmy blue is one of the smallest butterflies in the world. A fully grown pygmy blue is only as big as the tip of your finger!

The blue morpho is a dazzling butterfly. It is one of the largest butterflies in South America. The blue morpho drinks the juice of various fruits.

Fritillaries have tiny bristles on their front legs. These bristles are like brushes! They are used for cleaning the butterfly's feelers.

Magnificent moths

There are over 200,000 different kinds of moths. The satin moth's fuzzy white body makes it look as though it is wearing a fur coat!

The cecropia is one of the largest moths in North America. It can grow to be even bigger than the giant swallowtail butterfly!

The luna moth is a beautiful moth. It has long, graceful, light-green wings. Many people mistake it for a butterfly.

The hawk moth is a very fast flier. It can fly ten times as fast as you can walk—even if you walk quickly!

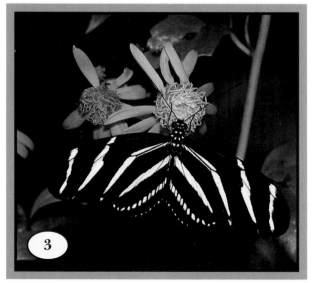

The name game

People have given butterflies and moths some interesting names. They may have looked at the pattern on the wings of one butterfly and said, "That looks just like a zebra." The butterflies and moths shown here are called: zebra butterfly, sunset moth, tiger swallowtail butterfly, hummingbird moth, and piano key butterfly.

5

4

Look at them carefully and decide which is which. The answers are in the box below.

1. Tiger swallowtail butterfly
2. Piano key butterfly
3. Zebra butterfly
4. Sunset moth
5. Hummingbird moth

Butterfly fun

It is fun to observe butterflies and moths in your own backyard. Keep a notebook and draw the ones you see. Look at each one's size, behavior, and the food it eats. Make notes of your findings. List reasons why you think moths and butterflies are an important part of nature.

Match the butterflies and moths you have seen with those in this book. You can also visit your library and find pictures in books called **field guides**. Field guides help identify birds, insects, and animals and tell you about their behavior.

Words to know

camouflage Patterns or colors that blend into the environment

chrysalis A cocoon

cocoon A covering that protects the pupa of an insect

hibernate To sleep through winter

metamorphosis The growing and changing from egg to adult

migrate To move a long distance from one place to another

mimic To resemble closely

nectar A sweet liquid made by flowers and used by bees in making honey

osmeterium A caterpillar's "horns"

pollen A fine, powdery material that comes from flowers

predator An animal that eats other animals

proboscis A long mouth tube used for sucking

prolegs The leglike stumps that help a caterpillar cling to twigs and leaves

Index

activities 28-30

butterflies 6, 7, 11, 19, 21, 24-25, 26, 29

camouflage 21

caterpillars 8, 9, 10-11, 13, 16, 18, 21

cocoons 9, 16

color 6, 15, 18-19, 21, 27

eating 12-13, 14, 16,

eggs 8, 22

eyes 15

eyespots 18

feelers 7, 14, 25

food 5, 6, 12-13, 14, 16, 30

hibernation 22

insects 5, 7, 12, 13, 21

life cycle 8-9

metamorphosis 8-9

migration 22-23

mimics 19, 21

monarch butterfly 19, 23

moths 6, 7, 8, 9, 18, 21, 26-27, 29

name game, the 29

poisonous butterflies and moths 18, 19, 29

pollen 5

predators 11, 16, 19, 21

proboscis 12, 14

pupa 8, 9

scales 5

senses 14-15

tongue 12

wings 5, 6, 9, 18, 21, 23, 27, 29

What is in the picture?

Here is some information about the photographs in this book.

page:	
front cover	A painted beauty butterfly
back cover	Luna moths live in southern parts of North America.
title page	Question mark butterflies are recognized by the silver edge on their wings.
4	A Malay lacewing butterfly
5	Polyphemus moths live in North and South America.
6	The cecropia moth is the largest moth in North America.
7	The front legs of the lavender fritillary are short and hairy.
8-9	These pictures show different stages in the metamorphosis of a cecropia moth.
10	Some people believe that if the black parts of a tiger moth caterpillar are short, the following winter will be short.
11 (top)	A cecropia moth caterpillar
11 (bottom)	A giant swallowtail butterfly caterpillar
12 (left)	An eastern black swallowtail butterfly
12 (right)	Hummingbird moths hover by beating their wings quickly.
13	A monarch butterfly caterpillar's bright colors tell enemies that it tastes bad.
14	The small apollo butterfly lives in western North America.
15	A cecropia moth
16	The spots on a sphinx moth caterpillar look like eyes.

page:	
17	A snake approaches a question mark butterfly.
18 (top)	A spicebush swallowtail butterfly caterpillar
18 (bottom)	A polyphemus moth
19 (top)	Monarch butterflies live almost everywhere in the world.
19 (bottom)	A viceroy butterfly
20	A hawk moth hides in the leaves.
21	This picture shows a giant swallowtail butterfly caterpillar with its osmeterium extended.
23	These monarch butterflies are covered in frost. The cool temperature helps them sleep.
24 (top)	Swallowtail butterflies are named after the long tail on their wings.
24 (bottom)	Pygmy blue butterflies live in Mexico and the southern United States.
25 (top)	Blue morpho butterflies live in the Amazon rainforest.
25 (bottom)	A fritillary butterfly
26 (top)	A satin moth
26 (bottom)	A cecropia moth
27 (top)	Luna moths can have a wingspan of 10 cm (4 inches).
27 (bottom)	Hawk moths have powerful wings.
28 (top)	Tiger swallowtail butterfly
28 (bottom left)	A piano key butterfly
28 (bottom right)	Zebra butterflies live in warm places.
29 (top)	A hummingbird moth
29 (bottom)	A sunset moth
30	This boy is attending a nature fair.

1 2 3 4 5 6 7 8 9 0   Printed in USA   3 2 1 0 9 8 7 6 5 4

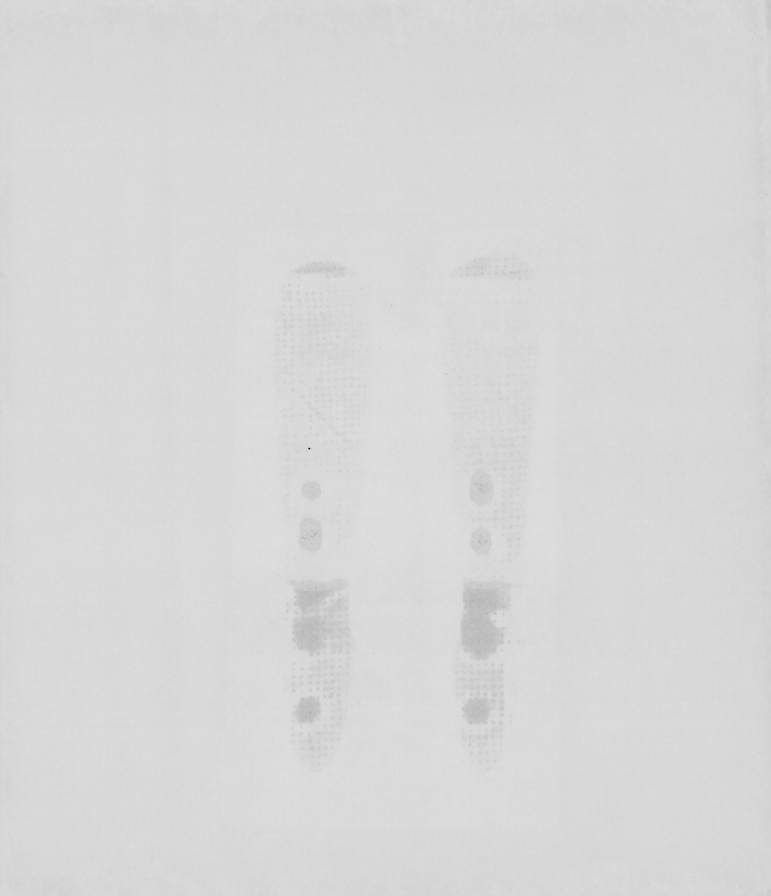